Lawrence stepped toward the elephant, his mind racing. If she charged, the electric fence would not stop her. He could be trampled. But this was their last chance. He looked up into her angry eyes. "Nana, please. Stay."

For my mother, Annalise Barrett,
with love, appreciation, and admiration.

© 2022 by Jennifer O'Connell

Hardcover ISBN 978-0-88448-928-3
Library of Congress Control Number 2022940580

10 9 8 7 6 5 4 3 2 1

Tilbury House Publishers • Thomaston, Maine
www.tilburyhouse.com

Illustrations created with acrylic paints on Strathmore Bristol paper
Illustration scans by Archival Arts Inc., Halethorpe, MD
Designed by Frame25 Productions
Printed in South Korea

Elephants
Remember

A True Story

Jennifer O'Connell

TILBURY HOUSE PUBLISHERS

Seven weeks earlier, 600 miles away . . . .

CRASH!!! Elephants spilled into the yard, crushing furniture, eating every plant in sight. Dogs howled. People shouted, "RUN!"

The troubled elephants had broken out of a nearby reserve. They had lost family members to poachers and been moved from place to place, and now no enclosure could contain them.

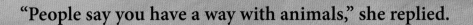

In a final effort to save them, a wildlife conservationist phoned Lawrence Anthony.

"Will you take the herd at your reserve?" she asked.

Elephants for free?! Lawrence couldn't believe it. "Why have you called me?"

"People say you have a way with animals," she replied.

Lawrence had grown up running barefoot through the bush. Now he owned Thula Thula, a wild-animal reserve in Zululand.

"We would welcome a herd but don't have electric fences," he said. "And the herd would attract poachers."

"We're out of options," she said. "If you can't take them, the elephants will have to be shot."

"*What?!*" Lawrence cried. "Bring them to Thula Thula. We'll give them a home!"

He hired villagers to string electric wires along the reserve's 20-mile fence. They also built a boma, or pen, to hold the elephants until they became used to their new surroundings and could be released into the reserve.

Then Lawrence received terrible news. While the rangers were rounding up the herd, the matriarch and her calf tried to escape and were shot and killed.

Lawrence was heartsick. *How will the herd ever calm down after that?* The next oldest elephant became the herd's new matriarch. She roared as the truck carried them away.

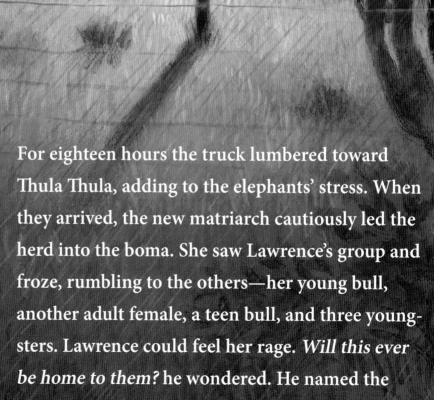

For eighteen hours the truck lumbered toward
Thula Thula, adding to the elephants' stress. When
they arrived, the new matriarch cautiously led the
herd into the boma. She saw Lawrence's group and
froze, rumbling to the others—her young bull,
another adult female, a teen bull, and three young-
sters. Lawrence could feel her rage. *Will this ever
be home to them?* he wondered. He named the
matriarch Nana, in honor of his mother.

ZAP!!! Nana jerked back from the electric fence, then traced her trunk close to the wires surrounding the pen. *She's feeling for weak spots!*

The elephants stood restlessly at the fence, facing north, the direction of their home.

In the morning, they were gone! They had crushed the boma fence with an uprooted tree, then smashed through the reserve's outer enclosure. "We have to find them!" cried Lawrence. "They'll be shot!"

All day long the men followed a trail of broken branches while a friend searched from his helicopter, but the herd was miles away.

After days of searching,
the pilot radioed, "I see them!" He swooped
down to try to force the elephants back toward
Thula Thula, but they bunched together and wouldn't
move, then vanished into a dark tangle of trees.

As the moon rose, Nana and her herd continued north and broke into another reserve. Smelling food in the rangers' hut, they pushed through the door and shattered windows. Then they tore open sacks of corn meal and sucked up the corn with their trunks.

"Help!" a ranger radioed.
"Elephants!"

The next morning when the conservation manager arrived, one of the herd trumpeted and charged. The man jumped in his jeep and barely escaped.

"These elephants are too dangerous. They must be destroyed," the rangers told Lawrence.

"They're confused and upset," Lawrence said. "And they haven't hurt anyone."

"Not YET!" said the rangers.

"Please," Lawrence begged. "Give us one more chance."

The rangers finally agreed. "But if they escape again, they will all be shot."

At dawn the helicopter hovered overhead again, a ranger with an air gun stationed at its open door. Nana hurried the elephants toward some nearby trees, but the ranger shot each of them with a tranquilizer dart. The sleeping elephants were hoisted onto trucks and driven back to Thula Thula.

Back in the boma, Nana screeched with fury. "This will never work unless she trusts someone," Lawrence told Thula Thula's head ranger.

Could that person be me? Lawrence decided to stay with the herd until he found out. There were no other options.

The elephants paced and shrieked as the two men set up camp. Later, when darkness fell, the herd became quiet. The men nodded off.

"Look!"

Lawrence jolted awake. The ranger pointed
to the boma, where Nana and the herd were
standing at the north fence. *They're about
to escape again!* Heart racing, Lawrence
slipped out of the car and stepped through
the bushes toward the herd.

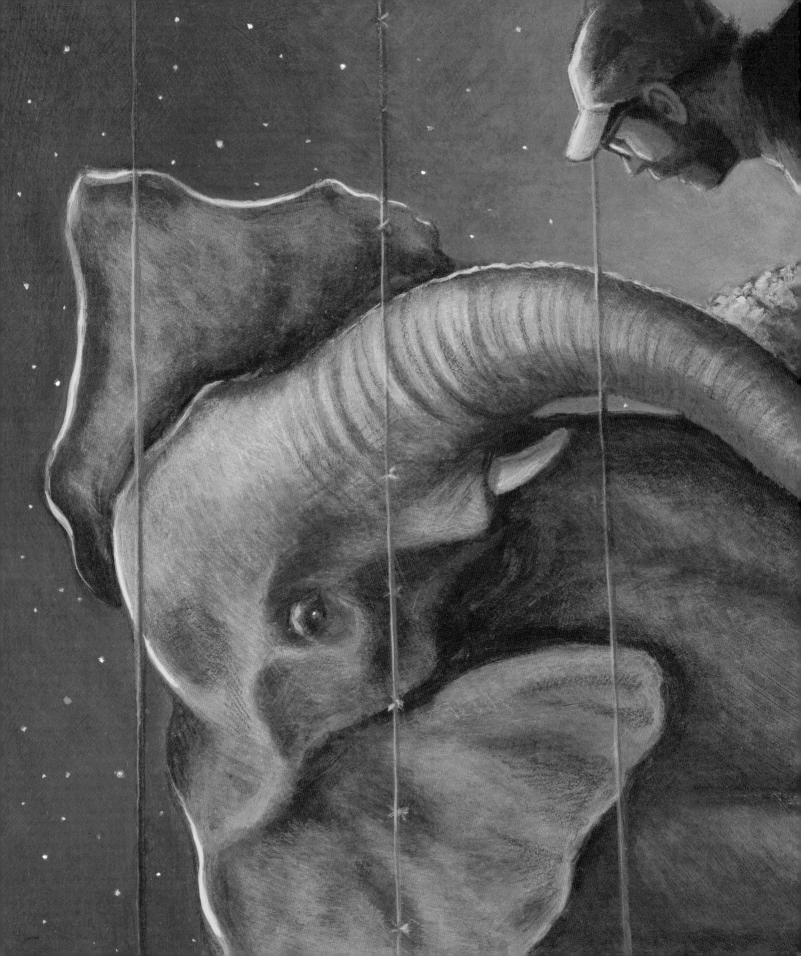

"Nana, please. Stay. You'll all be killed out there."

Nana moved toward him.

He knew she could charge through the fence and trample him. "Please, Nana." She glared down at him. "This can be your home. You'll be safe here."

Something in her eyes shifted. *What was that?*

Then she turned and led the herd back into the brush.

As the sun rose, Nana saw Lawrence and bellowed.

"Good morning!" he said, cheerfully. She cracked her ears at him. Later, as the men heaved alfalfa bales into the boma, Nana charged the fence, stopping just short of it.

"Don't you want food?" Lawrence asked. She kicked the dirt. "This can be your home now," he said. Nana roared.

Every day Lawrence stayed as close as the elephants would allow.
He told them stories and secrets. Every night, he begged Nana to stay.

As days turned to weeks, Nana came to know Lawrence's scent of coffee and sweat. In the past, humans had hit her, screamed at her . . . .

Lawrence sang folk songs to her. And when Nana
rumbled softly back to him, he listened.

One morning, Lawrence awoke to a rumbling that vibrated in his chest. Nana stood with her young bull right next to his camp!

What's this?

Nana's ears were down, relaxed. As Lawrence walked over, her trunk weaved through the fence. Lawrence paused, his heart pounding. If he stepped closer, Nana could grab him, hurt him . . . .

That's when he knew. The herd was ready to be released into the reserve! The next morning, Lawrence turned off the boma's electric fence and opened the gate. Nana walked up to the opening, sniffed, and stopped.

Why stop? Lawrence wondered.

She placed her trunk against the gate post and pushed it over easily, making room for her young bull to step around the deep puddle at the opening. Nana flapped her ears to signal "Follow me!" and the herd rushed down to the river.

After that day, Lawrence checked on the elephants regularly.
Sometimes he sensed their presence before he saw them.

How could that be? he'd wonder.

Nana often caught his scent and hurried over to greet him.

The herd visited Lawrence and his wife, Françoise, at their home on the reserve. When the elephants ate Françoise's vegetable garden, Lawrence built a fence around it.

Sometimes when Lawrence was away on a trip, the elephants waited near his house to greet him when he returned.

How did they know when I was coming back? he thought.

As years passed, word spread of Lawrence and the herd.
New elephants arrived. Births were celebrated.

Deaths were mourned.

The original herd of seven grew to twenty-one, forming two herds. More people came to see them and to stay at Thula Thula's lodge. Eventually, Lawrence began to distance himself from the elephants. He wanted them to remain wild and alert, safe from poachers. They would be in danger if they trusted all people.

But Lawrence and Nana continued to meet secretly.

"My baba," he called her.

One day, sad news arrived at Thula Thula. While away on a trip, Lawrence had suffered a heart attack and died. Calls, emails, and messages flooded in. Françoise was stunned by her husband's sudden death but determined to keep Thula Thula operating—for Lawrence and for their shared dream of protecting animals.

Two days later, a ranger radioed
Françoise at the Main House.
"Look outside!" he told her excitedly.

Led by Nana, the elephants had come from miles
away, across the reserve. They stood at the edge of
the yard, rumbling quietly.

And for the next two years they returned to Lawrence and Françoise's house on the same day, at the same time.

Because elephants remember.

What do elephants feel?

Elephants mourn the deaths of their family members. In 2012, when all of Thula Thula's elephants walked twelve miles across the reserve to Lawrence's home after he died, they were clearly distressed. They had not been there for many months. No one knows how the elephants knew that Lawrence had died.

Who was Lawrence Anthony?

Lawrence Anthony fell in love with the South African bush as a boy. In 1998 he and Françoise purchased a large swath of land in Zululand, which became the Thula Thula Private Game Reserve. Lawrence was a passionate conservationist, committed to preserving the land, protecting the animals that lived there, and involving the people of Zululand in these efforts.

When he was first approached to provide a home for the troubled elephant herd, Lawrence was thrilled because elephants had not been in his area for more than a century. But he had no experience with elephants, and Thula Thula wasn't set up for them. When he learned that the herd would be killed if he declined to take it, he embraced the challenge. That was Lawrence.

He was told by elephant experts that humans should stay away from the boma pen to keep the elephants feral (wild) and enable them to settle. But when the herd broke out and showed that they would continue to escape, Lawrence realized that he'd have to try a different approach if he was going to save them. Little did he know that he would win the trust of Nana and the other elephants, changing him forever.

When Lawrence became known as "the elephant whisperer" he responded, "It was they who whispered to me, and taught me how to listen." Lawrence's story inspires us to "listen" to other beings—people and animals, who are different from us—and to listen to our own true voice, deep within ourselves.

Why was Nana the new matriarch?

Herds are made up of six to twelve female adult elephants, usually a grandmother, her adult daughters, and their male and female calves. The oldest, most experienced elephant is usually the leader, or matriarch. Her extensive memory of places to find water and food is crucial to the herd's survival. If she becomes sick or dies, the next oldest sister or daughter usually steps in as the new leader, as Nana did when the herd arrived at Thula Thula in 1999.

Why were electric fences needed?

Electric fences are meant to startle but not hurt large animals such as elephants. Since elephants are so strong, they can push through most fences, but if they get a shock when they touch a fence, they usually back off and stay within the enclosure.

Why did Lawrence need to toss bales of alfalfa into the boma?

Depending on their size, adult elephants eat up to 400 pounds of plant matter (leaves, bark, grasses, and fruit) *each day*. They poop as much as 300 pounds of dung in a day! There was not nearly enough vegetation in the temporary boma pen for the herd to eat.

Why was it dangerous for Lawrence to step closer to Nana's trunk?

An elephant's trunk is part nose and part upper lip and contains more than 40,000 muscles. A trunk can weigh up to 300 pounds and can uproot big trees and toss enemies in the air or crush them.

Elephants can also use the tips of their trunks to pick small berries. They drink with their trunks by sucking up water and then squirting it into their mouths. They also spray themselves with water to cool off. They have a keen sense of smell and, when swimming underwater, raise their trunks like a snorkel tube above the surface to breathe.

How do elephants communicate with one another?

Elephants can trumpet, roar, grunt, rumble, purr, shriek, and scream to express what they are feeling and to "talk" with one another. Elephants' rumbles are like a drumming sound made in their throat. These sounds can be so low that human ears cannot hear the "infrasounds," but elephants can, sometimes up to six miles away. Elephants can also use their feet and trunks to feel the ground and understand vibrations or "seismic signals" created by loud rumbles from other elephants many miles away. Elephants use their trunks to touch and communicate with other elephants. They also use their ears and body movements to convey meaning.

Do elephants celebrate births?

The birth of a calf is a joyful and exciting event for the herd. All the elephants touch and caress the newborn with their trunks, welcoming the new family member. Whenever a calf was born at Thula Thula, the herd would bring the baby elephant to the edge of Lawrence and Françoise's yard to proudly introduce the new family member. When Lawrence's first grandson was born, he showed the baby to the herd!

Who was Lawrence's dog?

Max, an energetic Staffordshire bull terrier, was Lawrence's constant companion. He was well trained, loyal and fearless. Lawrence said that he was "the perfect bush dog." When Lawrence commanded Max to lie down and stay, often for the dog's safety, he would instantly obey. Lawrence was very sad when Max died.

Is there poaching at Thula Thula?

Yes, poaching is a constant threat to the animals at Thula Thula. Many animals are killed for their meat. Elephants are killed for their ivory tusks, which are teeth that grow out of each side of the elephant's upper jaw. The ivory is then sold illegally to be used for jewelry and decorative objects. Buying ivory endangers elephants as it encourages poaching.

How is Thula Thula operating today?

Lawrence's wife, Françoise Malby-Anthony, and a dedicated staff have kept Thula Thula thriving. In 2021, the reserve merged with the neighboring Lavoni and Zulweni game reserves to create the Greater Zululand Wildlife Conservancy. With more than 13,837 acres, its herds have increased to 28 elephants.

Françoise also founded and operates the South African Conservation Fund, the official nonprofit organization of Thula Thula. This organization sponsors a center for orphaned and wounded wildlife and a volunteer camp where people can come to live and learn about conservation, the African bush, and ways to help our planet.

Author's Note

When I read about Thula Thula's elephants mysteriously appearing at the Anthonys' home after Lawrence's death, I wanted to learn more about Lawrence's unique connection with Nana and the elephants. His book, *The Elephant Whisperer*, well describes his bravery, creative problem solving, and compassion.

Lawrence knew and named every elephant at Thula Thula, but his first and strongest relationship was with Nana, the matriarch. Their friendship is the focus of this story.

There is still much to learn about elephants and the other animals with whom we share our planet. It would be a real and preventable tragedy if these sensitive and sentient beings disappear forever. We must all do our part to make sure they survive. Their fate is in our hands.

Acknowledgments

I am grateful to Françoise Malby-Anthony for her generous research assistance. Lawrence Anthony's *The Elephant Whisperer* (with Graham Spence) and Françoise Malby-Anthony's sequel, *An Elephant in My Kitchen* (with Katja Willemsen) served as valuable resources.

To learn more about the Thula Thula Private Game Reserve and the South African Conservation Fund visit ThulaThula.com and SAConservation.fund.

A portion of the royalties for this book will be
contributed to the South African Conservation Fund.

Additional Resources

Anthony, Lawrence, with Graham Spence, adapted for young readers by Thea Feldman. *The Elephant Whisperer*. Henry Holt and Company, 2017.

Bove, Jennifer. *I Wish I Was an Elephant*. Harper, 2018.

Desmond, Jenni. *The Elephant*. Enchanted Lion Books, 2018.

Firestone, Mary. *Top 50 Reasons To Care About Elephants*. Enslow Publishers, Inc., 2010.

Joubert, Beverly and Dereck. *Face to Face With Elephants*. National Geographic, 2008.

Morgan, Jody. *Elephant Rescue: Changing the Future for Endangered Wildlife*. Firefly Books, 2004.

O'Connell, Caitlin. *The Elephant Scientist*. Houghton Mifflin Harcourt, 2011.

Moss, Cynthia. *Elephant Woman*. Atheneum Books For Young Readers, 1997.

Pringle, Laurence. *Elephants! Strange and Wonderful*, Boyds Mills Press, 2021.

Roy, Katherine. *How to Be an Elephant: Growing Up in the African Wild*. David Macaulay Studio, Roaring Book Press, 2017.

Websites

David Sheldrick Wildlife Trust: SheldrickWildlifeTrust.org

The International Elephant Foundation: ElephantConservation.org

Save The Elephants: SaveTheElephants.org

World Wildlife Fund: WorldWildLife.org